CLASSIFYING LIVING THINGS

Darlene R. Stille

Science consultant: Suzy Gazlay, M.A.,
science curriculum resource teacher

Please visit our web site at: www.garethstevens.com
For a free color catalog describing Gareth Stevens Publishing's list
of high-quality books, call 1-800-542-2595 (USA)
or 1-800-387-3178 (Canada).

Library of Congress Cataloging-in-Publication Data

Stille, Darlene R.
    Classifying living things / Darlene Stille. — North American ed.
        p. cm. — (Gareth Stevens vital science: Life science)
    Includes bibliographical references and index.
    ISBN-13: 978-0-8368-8438-8 — ISBN-10: 0-8369-8438-8 (lib. bdg.)
    ISBN-13: 978-0-8368-8447-0 — ISBN-10: 0-8368-8447-7 (softcover)
    1. Biology—Classification.   I. Title.
    QH83.S77   2008
    578.01'2—dc22   2007021475

This edition first published in 2008 by
Gareth Stevens Publishing
A Weekly Reader® Company
1 Reader's Digest Road
Pleasantville, NY 10570-7000 USA

Editor: Honor Head
Design, illustrations, and image search: Q2a Media
Cover design: Q2a Media

Gareth Stevens art direction: Tammy West
Gareth Stevens graphic designer: Dave Kowalski
Gareth Stevens production: Jessica Yanke
Gareth Stevens science curriculum consultant: Suzy Gazlay, M.A.

Photo credits: t=top, b=bottom, m=middle, l=left, r=right
Oxford Scientific Films/photolibrary: Half title, 13, 37tr; Elenathewise/Dreamstime: 5, 33tr; Nikolay
Starchenko/Shutterstock: 6bl; WizData, inc./Shutterstock: 7tl; Photolibrary (Australia): 9b; Tan
Wei Ming/Shuttestock: 10tr; Photo Researchers, Inc./photolibrary: 14tl, 36t; Moondigger/Creative
Commons Attribution ShareAlike 2.5: 15; J. Norman Reid/Shutterstock: 16br; Michaela Steininger/
Shutterstock: 19t; David Rose/iStockphoto: 19m; Kenneth Sponsler/Shutterstock: 19b; EML/
Shutterstock: 20b; Phil Sigin/iStockphoto: 23; sgame/Shutterstock: 24tl; Eimantas Buzas/
Shutterstock: 25tr; Larsek/Shutterstock: 29t1; Ooyoo/iStockphoto: 29t2; George Clerk/
iStockphoto:29t3, Phototake Inc./Photolibrary: 29t4, 29t5, 35tl; Eric Isselée/iStockphoto: 30bl;
Nathan Menifee/iStockphoto: 30br; Nate89/Dreamstime: 31bl; Spanishalex/Dreamstime: 31br;
Makarov Vladyslav/Shutterstock: 33bl1; Jasenka/Dreamstime: 33bl2; Haveseen/Dreamstime: 33bl3;
Stuart Pitkin/iStock: 38b.

Every effort has been made to trace the copyright holders for the photos used in this book.
The publisher apologizes, in advance, for any unintentional omissions and would be pleased
to insert the appropriate acknowledgments in any subsequent edition of this publication.

Printed in the United States of America

1 2 3 4 5 6 7 8 9 11 10 09 08 07

Contents

1 Living or Nonliving?

The world is filled with all kinds of things. Some things are natural, such as a snow-capped mountain and all the animals and plants that live there. A dog romping through a backyard full of colorful flowers is another natural scene—as is a clear stream filled with flashes of fish swimming by.

Other things are made by human beings. Big things such as buildings, airplanes and city streets. Other man-made things are smaller—cans of beans and loaves of bread, a pair of shoes, a computer, magazines, and books.

Some things are living or were once alive, such as fossils. Some things are nonliving and were never alive, like a brick. How can we tell the difference?

Signs of life

Biologists have identified several basic signs of life. Anything that is considered alive must have all of these characteristics.

Motion They must show some kind of motion. Many living things move around. Most animals and the tiny, one-celled organisms seen under a microscope move around. We might not think of other living things as moving around. For example,

The living and nonliving exist side by side. Parks with grass and flowers make city centers filled with man-made structures better places to live.

plants have branches and leaves that sway in the wind, but a plant cannot take up its roots and walk away. Tiny holes in leaves, however, open and close to let gases in and out. Even animals that settle in one place and never leave show motion. Coral animals that build and live on limestone reefs do not seem to move. Yet they have tentacles that they can move around in the water to catch passing prey. Even if an organism does not seem to move at all,

A bounding dog moves on its own over a short distance very quickly.

there is motion inside—the motion takes place inside the organism's cells.

Cells A living thing must be made of cells. Cells are the basic building blocks of all life. Large organisms are made of billions of cells. Small organisms can contain as few as one cell. Amoebas, for example, are one-celled organisms.

Food and energy A living thing, no matter how many cells it has, must be able to make energy from food. Plants make their own food from sunlight, water, and a gas in the air called carbon dioxide. This process is called photosynthesis. Animals eat plants or other animals as their food. Single-cell organisms take in food from their surroundings. Living things use this energy to make the chemicals they need for life and to move these chemicals around in their cells. Living things give off waste products from the

Baby birds rely completely on their parents for food. In a few weeks, they are on their own.

process of using energy. One of the waste products that animals give off is carbon dioxide. One of the waste products that plants give off is oxygen.

Growth and reproduction All living organisms must grow and develop. They must also be able to reproduce or make copies of themselves. Most living organisms need another similar organism to reproduce. Some organisms, such as one-celled animals

and certain plants, can reproduce without the help of another. For example, a one-celled animal might simply split in half. A completely new plant can sometimes grow from one leaf.

Senses and responses Living things must be aware of the world around them. They must be able to sense their environment and respond to changes in their environment. Animals can sense heat and cold. They can feel pain. Dogs, insects, and even earthworms move away from danger. People put on sweaters and jackets when cold winter winds blow. Plants can sense light and dark. Some flower petals

🔑 Pronunciation Key: ◣

amoeba *(ah-ME-bah)*
carbohydrate
(kar-bow-HIGH-drate)
photosynthesis
(foe-toe-SIN-thuh-sis)

7

Exploding a Myth

Until the 1600s, people thought that life could spring from nonliving substances. This was called "spontaneous generation." Italian doctor Francesco Redi believed that only living things could produce living things. In 1668, he set up an experiment to find out for sure. It was probably the first scientific research. At that time, people often found maggots in their meat. Redi believed maggots did not magically appear. He thought maggots were the early stage in the life cycle of flies. He put meat in jars and set them outside. One set of jars had no lids. The second set was covered with gauze. The third set had tight lids. Redi stated that maggots would not appear in the closed jars. He was right! Other scientists also proved this.

close up when the Sun goes down. Even one-celled creatures can sense changes in their environment. For example, if water becomes very salty, the one-celled organisms will try to move away to less-salty areas.

Adaptations Individual plants and animals sometimes need to change slightly to survive. The change, or adaptation, occurs only in that plant or animal. It will not be passed on to offspring. The adaptation improves the life of that particular organism. We say the plant or animal has adapted to its environment.

For instance, a plant that is shaded by others cannot move into the sunlight. Instead, it may grow a few extra-long branches. These longer branches reach beyond the shade into sunlight. This shaded plant will not die off. It has adapted to its location.

Signs of Life in Nonliving Things

Some nonliving things show characteristics of living things. Some nonliving things move, but they move because of another force. Our Moon and Earth orbit, or move around, each other as both orbit the Sun. Asteroids and other space rocks also move around. The force of gravity causes objects to move in space. The blades of an electric fan spin around, but the fan is not alive. Electric current causes the motion in the fan.

Waves of water lap a sandy beach. The water moves, but it is not alive. Wind blowing on the surface and currents in the water make the motion of the waves.

The rock that makes up mountains can slide downhill, but it does not move on its own. Rock is made of minerals. Pebbles and clay are also made of minerals. Many nonliving natural things or those made by people contain a lot of minerals. Minerals are nonliving things.

Some minerals can appear in crystal form. Crystals may also form when certain liquids evaporate. Look at

Winds and currents cause waves to move through water and break upon the beaches.

a crystal using a microscope. You will see regular, repeating patterns. Crystals form because of the way the atoms of that substance line up.

A crystal can grow in size, but it is not alive. It never moves on its own. It cannot adapt. Crystals form or enlarge only under certain conditions. For example, snowflakes need just the right weather to form. Snowflakes are crystals that appear when air temperature and humidity allow them to form.

The Chemicals of Life

Bones and seashells are organic substances. They are formed by living organisms. Living and nonliving things are made of different materials. All living things contain the element carbon. Carbon joins with atoms of other elements to make molecules. Molecules that contain carbon atoms

Crystals are made of nonliving, inorganic minerals.

are called organic molecules. The material that makes up living things is called organic material.

The material of things that were never alive is called inorganic material. Inorganic material does not contain carbon. Living things, however, can contain minerals and other inorganic materials, just as nonliving things do.

Organic molecules are the chemicals of life. Organic molecules in all living things come together to create cells. Cells, in turn, produce a

10

range of proteins. Proteins are responsible for what an organism looks like and how it functions. Proteins called enzymes speed up chemical reactions in cells. Proteins called hormones regulate many systems in animals and plants. Fats and carbohydrates in food are also organic molecules. The fats and carbohydrates are "burned" in animal cells to provide energy. Protein in food gets broken down by the digestive system into chemicals called amino acids. Amino acids are used by the cells to assemble new proteins.

One of the most important chemicals of life is an acid called DNA (deoxyribonucleic acid). This is the molecule of which genes are made. All the cells of living things, no matter how big or small, contain DNA. DNA is the blueprint of life. It carries the code for making every protein that an organism needs. It enables the organism to grow and reproduce.

Oil Was Once Alive

The gasoline that flows from the gas pump into a car is not alive. The oil that powers factory machinery or heats homes is not alive. Yet oil and gasoline are made of molecules that contain carbon and another element, hydrogen. These molecules are called hydrocarbons. Oil and gas are not alive today, but they came from things that were once alive. Millions of years ago, prehistoric plants and animals died and were buried deep underground. Over time, this once-living matter changed into natural gas, oil, and coal, which we burn as fuel today. Because they came from prehistoric organisms, these fuels are called fossil fuels.

2 Needs and Living Things

All living things have basic needs. They need food and water, for example. They need gases in the air or water to breathe. Many organisms need shelter from extreme weather conditions or protection from enemies.

Needs affect how living things behave. Spiders weave webs to trap flies or other insects for food. A tiger uses its speed and strength to stalk and kill prey. A fox makes a den in a small cave to give shelter to her young. Birds and butterflies migrate across great distances in the spring and fall in search of food and warmth.

Most animals also have behaviors that attract mates. Male and female fireflies flash mating codes to one another on summer nights. Male whooping cranes flap their wings as they dance for females. The male of a certain spider species will present a trapped insect to a female spider.

Needs and Appearance

Needs can affect how organisms look. Giraffes have long necks so that they can reach leaves near the tops of trees. Flowers have bright colors to attract bees and other insects, which pick up and carry

Many spider species weave delicate-looking webs for catching insects. Spider silk is very strong for its weight.

The Journey of the Monarch Butterflies

Millions of monarchs journey to southern forests for the winter.

Monarch butterflies make an amazing journey each year. The journey covers thousands of miles (kilometers) from places in the northern United States and Canada to places as far as southern California and even central Mexico. This is quite a feat for a creature that meaures about 4 inches (10 centimeters) wide from wingtip to wingtip and weighs less than half an ounce (0.01 kilogram).

Not all monarch butterflies make this long trip. The butterflies usually only live four to eight weeks. Each year, however, they produce a super generation in late summer or early autumn. These "super monarchs" live for seven or eight months—the equivalent of a human being living for more than five hundred years!

Their lifespan allows them to make the journey and spend the winter in the south. Hundreds of monarchs crowd together and hang from trees. They enter a state similar to hibernation to conserve energy. In spring, they fly north again. They look for milkweed plants, the only food that monarchs eat. Along the way, the butterflies reproduce and die.

Their offspring, however, continue their northward journey, living their normal four to eight weeks until the summer ends. Then another super generation is born to make the trip again.

A flounder is a master of camouflage.

pollen to other flowers so the flowering plants can reproduce. Camouflage and mimicry are used by some animals for protection. Many fish have dark-colored backs and light bellies so that it is more difficult for enemies to see them from above and below. An insect called a katydid uses camouflage to look like a leaf. Using mimicry, the wings of the viceroy butterfly look like the brown, white, and orange wings of the monarch butterfly, which gets an unpleasant taste from feeding on milkweed. Such mimicry can protect the viceroy from being eaten by birds that have experienced the monarch's bad taste.

Needs and Adaptations

Living things behave and look the way they do because living things can adapt when their environment changes. Groups of living things can evolve, or develop new characteristics that allow them to survive and reproduce. These changes occur because of changes in their genes. Their offspring reproduce and pass the beneficial changes to their offspring. In this way, changes in genes allow evolution to occur.

Changes in genes are called mutations. Some mutations are harmful. For example, cancer is caused by a harmful change in one or more genes. Some

mutations are beneficial. Suppose the climate in an area becomes drier. Plants with genes that allow them to store water more efficiently will survive. These plants will pass their

Cactus have adapted to desert living. Their thick skins swell with stored water after a rain.

16

beneficial genes on to their offspring. The others will die out. Cactus plants with thick stems that hold water for months evolved in this way.

Over hundreds of millions of years, such adaptations led to a great diversity of living things. From one simple, single-cell life form that appeared on Earth about 3.5 billion years ago, tens of millions of different kinds of organisms have evolved.

Some fish, for example, evolved because groups of organisms adapted to live in ocean water. Other organisms adapted to live on dry land. Land animals evolved into worms, dinosaurs, birds, insects, and mammals.

🔑 Pronunciation Key:

camouflage (*KAH-meh-flahz*)
hibernation (*HIGH-bur-NAY-shun*)
mutation (*myu-TAY-shun*)

Fossils and Extinct Organisms

Many kinds of organisms that once lived have died out, or become extinct. Scientists can learn about extinct organisms that lived millions of years ago because some of these organisms were preserved as fossils. Conditions have to be just right for a fossil to form. The organism must quickly be buried by mud to keep it from decaying or being destroyed by other means. Over millions of years, the fossil forms as mud hardens to rock or minerals replace the organism's body parts. Over millions of more years wind or water erode away the top layers of rock to expose the fossil. There are many kinds of fossils, such as stone casts of bones, teeth, animal footprints, and leaves.

3 Sorting It Out

Thousands of years ago there were no scientists in the way we think of scientists. Scientific methods of observing, forming hypotheses, and testing hypotheses with experiments had not yet been developed. People who thought about the natural world and how it worked were called philosophers.

The philosophers observed many kinds of living things. They saw that plants were different from animals. They saw that bugs were different from dogs.

Philosophers who lived in ancient Greece realized the need for a way of sorting out the various kinds of living things. They began to work on a way of naming and organizing, or classifying, all the different kinds of living things. This kind of classification is called taxonomy. Some ways of grouping help biologists understand how different organisms evolved over time.

How To Sort

All things, living or nonliving, can be sorted into groups, or categories, based on characteristics. Think about what you did when you had to clean up your room. You may have sorted out clothing from books and games. You

Living things can be sorted into groups,
such as animals (top) or plants (middle).
The groups are then sorted into smaller
groups, such as birds (bottom).

may have sorted your clothing by type. Socks went into drawers. Shirts or blouses and jeans were placed on hangers in the closet.

Things can be classified by any of their characteristics. Suppose you have a box of blue, red, and yellow beads with different shapes. You can sort the beads in different ways. You could sort them into groups by color. You could sort them by shapes, such as square or round. Groups of colors or shapes can be sorted by other characteristics. For example, all the beads that are red and round can be sorted into one group. All the square yellow beads can be sorted into another group.

In the same way, taxonomists look for characteristics that living things have in common. They use these characteristics to sort living things into many different groups.

Why Sort?

Human beings have a need to put things in order. Things that are in order are easier to find. If pencils are separated by color it is easier to find a red pencil than it would be if hundreds of pencils of different colors were thrown together in a drawer.

Things that are in order look neater. Books grouped on a shelf look neater than books thrown all over a room. The books on a shelf may also be analyzed. If they are sorted by fiction, nonfiction,

Macaques monkeys belong to the same Order as chimpanzees, gorillas, and humans—primates.

or author's name, it is easy to count how many kinds of each book there are.

Biologists also have a need to sort things. Nature is a jumble of ants, oak trees, robins, roses, bees, worms, snakes, blue jays, grass, tigers, sheep, butterflies, and thousands of other living things.

Biologists group different organisms together because they are easier to find when they are grouped in their proper place. Grouping helps scientists compare the traits of different organisms and helps them to better understand how organisms work together in an ecosystem. It also helps scientists understand how one organism is related to another.

🔑 Pronunciation Key:

hypotheses (*high-PAH-thuh-seez*)
philosophers (*fi-LAH-si-ferz*)
virus (*VEYE-ris*)

Are Viruses Living Things?

Viruses infect, or get inside of, living things. Some viruses infect animals and others infect plants. There are even viruses that infect bacteria. Many viruses cause diseases in humans. Colds and flu are among the most common diseases caused by viruses. AIDS is also caused by a virus called HIV. Viruses have characteristics of both living and nonliving things. Viruses contain genes, but viruses cannot live and reproduce on their own. They cannot even make their own energy. When viruses invade the cells of living things, the genes of the virus direct the cell to make copies of the virus. The viruses then burst out of the cell and infect other cells.

Scientists do not classify viruses as living organisms.

21

4 How Taxonomy Developed

The word "taxonomy" comes from two Greek words. "Taxis" is a Greek word that means arrangement. "Nomos" is a Greek word that means law. Together they mean "law of arrangement." Taxonomy is the set of rules for arranging or grouping things.

One of the first taxonomists was the Greek philosopher Aristotle, who lived in the 300s B.C. Aristotle made careful observations of living things and devised one of the first classification systems. To create this system, Aristotle needed some rules for sorting out living things. Aristotle was a very logical thinker. He thought it was logical to choose complexity as his basic sorting-out rule. He grouped all living things according to whether their structure was simple or complex. The simplest animals were small and lacked backbones. Earthworms, for example, he grouped as simple animals. The most complex organisms were human beings. In this scheme, or ladder of life, each organism had its permanent rung.

Aristotle divided all living things into two groups, animals and plants. He was much more interested in animals than plants.

In the fourth century B.C., ancient Greek philosopher Aristotle (384–322 B.C.) created one of the first classification systems.

He divided all animals into two other groups, those with red blood and those without red blood. Aristotle's red-blooded group is basically the same as animals with backbones, or vertebrates. His group lacking red blood is much the same as the group lacking backbones, or invertebrates.

Aristotle subdivided the red-blooded (vertebrate) group into four-footed animals that

The World of "Animalcules."

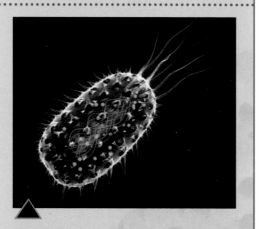

One-celled organisms can only be seen through a microscope.

The first microscopes may have been made by Dutch eyeglass makers in the late 1500s. They noticed that putting two lenses in a tube made things viewed through it look a lot bigger. It took almost 100 years for another Dutchman, Anton van Leeuwenhoek, to discover the tiny living world visible only through microscopes. In 1674, he saw tiny "animalcules" swimming around in drops of liquid.

give birth to live young (mammals), birds, four-footed animals that lay eggs (reptiles and amphibians), whales, and fish. He subdivided those without red blood (invertebrates) into cephalopoda (octopus, squid, and cuttlefish); weak-shelled animals (soft-shell crabs); hard-shelled animals (hard-shell clams, oysters, and snails); insects; spiders; centipedes; and various sea creatures—such as starfish and sea urchins.

Classification was simpler in Aristotle's day. Only about one thousand living things were known. His system was used for almost two thousand years. After Aristotle's time, however, people discovered many, many more organisms. For instance, some explorers from Europe found new organisms in North and South America, Africa, and Asia. To make things more complicated, early scientists realized fossils were remains of extinct living things. Then the invention of the microscope revealed a world of previously unseen organisms. As new living things were discovered, so a new classification system was going to be needed.

Groups of Groups

In the 1700s, Swedish scientist Carolus Linneaus developed a clever way to classify all living organisms. He sorted living things into groups of groups that shared common traits. Linneaus started by identifying general characteristics of the organisms. He classified those organisms into more specific groups. Each new group was set up according to common characteristics. The most specialized group contained only one specific organism.

🔑 Pronunciation Key:

animacules (AN-ih-ma-kules)
hierarchical *(high-err-ARK-ical)*
Leeuwenhoek (LEW-wen-hoak)

The Mule

A mule is produced by cross-breeding a donkey and a horse.

It does not happen often, but different species can breed with another. A mule is an example of cross-breeding. A mule is a cross between a male donkey and a female horse.

Mules were first bred as long as three thousand years ago. They can carry heavy loads for long distances over rough ground. A mule has a head like a horse and the long ears of a donkey.

25

For instance, to classify a certain type of tree, Linneaus first thought about all living organisms. Next, he separated plants from animals. He then separated trees from plants, then split trees into those with leaves and those with needles, and so on, until he ended with just one type of tree in a group.

Linneaus classified animals in a similar manner. He put animals with backbones in one group. Animals without backbones were put in another group. From there, each animal was placed in a more specific group according to its traits. Members of each new group shared more specialized characteristics. Again, the final classification group held just one type of animal.

Linneaus used seven groupings for each organism. He labeled his groups Kingdom, Phylum, Class, Order, Family, Genus, and Species. Using this method, every single organism ends

up in a unique group. This orderly classification system is known as taxonomy.

An easy way to remember the taxonomy classification system is by memorizing this sentence: King Philip Came Over For Grape Slushies. The first letter of each word represents the Kingdom, Phylum, Class, Order, Family, Genus, and Species. The Genus and Species names are always italicized. The Genus name is also always capitalized. The species name is not capitalized.

You might use Linneaus's system to set up a taxonomy chart for your school (Kingdom). Divide the school into grades (Phyla). Next, divide the grades into classrooms (Class). Each classroom is devoted to only one subject (Order). That subject is covered in one textbook (Family). The book has many chapters (Genus). Each chapter concentrates on one unique topic (Species).

Linnaeus and His System

Carl von Linné loved to walk in the fields near his home in Rashult, Sweden, where he was born in 1707. He spent all his time collecting specimens of plants and carefully studying them. His friends and family nicknamed him "the little botanist." In addition to botany, he loved Latin. He changed his name to its Latin form, Carolus Linnaeus.

When he was at Uppsala University in Sweden, Linnaeus met Olof Celsius, a teacher who encouraged him to become a botanist and helped him get a job at the university teaching botany.

In 1732, Linnaeus went on a trip to collect plants in Lapland, which is north of the Arctic Circle. He wrote books about his travels. He also wrote two books that listed all the plants and animals known in the world at that time.

Linnaeus saw the need for a system of classifying all these plants and animals. He developed a system with numerous classification levels. In Linnaeus's system, every species had a two-part name in Latin. No two species were allowed to have the same official scientific name.

Linnaeus had many scientific interests. He became a doctor and practiced medicine for a short time. He returned to botany and to his lifelong interest in classifying things. After classifying plants and animals, he used his system to classify minerals and even some diseases.

His work and his books made him famous. He traveled to many countries to visit with other scientists. He became a respected professor of botany at the University in Uppsala. Linneaus died in 1778.

5 Inside the Kingdoms

Subspecies and Superorders

Sometimes an individual organism or group of organisms is different from others in its group —but not enough to be placed in another group. Taxonomists solved this problem by creating a division of a group such as Subphylum, Subclass, Superorder, Suborder, Superfamily, and Subfamily. Plants species that people have developed for their desirable characteristics are called cultivars.

Just as the number of known species changes, so do the classification systems. Linnaeus's first classification system divided all living things into two Kingdoms—plants and animals. As scientists found new species and studied known species more carefully, they realized the need for more Kingdoms, however.

During the 1900s, scientists classified living things into five Kingdoms: Animalia, Plantae, Fungi, Protista, and Monera. New tools for studying animals have shown that there should perhaps be six Kingdoms. The new tools employ methods that study genetic materials. These studies suggest that the Monera Kingdom should be divided into two Kingdoms.

The cheetah belongs to Kingdom Animalia.

A sunflower belongs to Kingdom Plantae.

A mushroom is part of an organism that belongs to Kingdom Fungi.

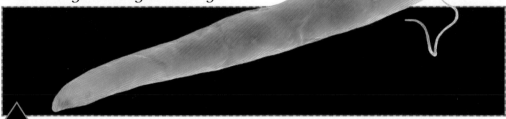

A Euglena belongs to Kingdom Protista.

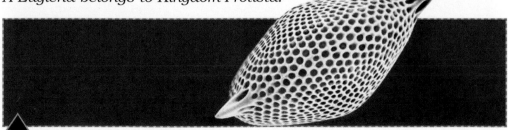

A saltwater radiolarian also belongs to Kingdom Protista.

Today, some scientists recognize five Kingdoms but others recognize six Kingdoms. Still others believe that information from genetic studies might one day call for a reorganization into seven or more Kingdoms.

Animalia, the Animal Kingdom

The Kingdom Animalia is the largest of all the kingdoms. There are about two million known animals. Most of those are insects. Animals are multicellular organisms that eat and digest food for energy, breathe in oxygen, and give off carbon dioxide as a waste product. More than thirty Phyla have been identified in the animal Kingdom. Some of the more familiar include: *Chordata*—animals with nerve chords, including vertebrates. *Arthropoda*—animals with three or more pairs of jointed legs, such as insects; spiders, mites, ticks, and other arachnids; crustaceans; millipedes and centipedes. *Echinodermata*—animals with radial symmetry and five arms, or parts, such as sea stars, sea cucumbers, sand dollars, and sea urchins.

A colorful bird

A patterned snake

Corals

A Queen Conch shell

Breeds of Dogs

A miniature poodle looks very different from a German shepherd or a great Dane.

Yet biologists classify all dogs as belonging to the same species. That is because poodles, German shepherds, and great Danes can all breed with one another. In fact, selective breeding over many centuries gave rise to the differences between dogs. Different kinds of dogs are called breeds.

There is another odd thing about dogs. They can breed with canines other than *Canis familiaris*. Dogs can breed with wolves, and their offspring can reproduce. This characteristic has led many biologists to question whether dogs should be classified as *Canis familiaris*. Perhaps, they suggest, the dog should be classified as *Canis lupis*, a gray wolf. The dog would then be a subspecies named *Canis lupis familiaris*. Dogs can also breed with coyotes and jackals, but this happens very rarely.

31

Annelida—segmented worms, such as earthworms and leeches.

Mollusca—animals with a bag-like mantle and a foot, such as octopuses, squids, bivalves, snails, and cuttlefish.

Nematoda—roundworms, worm-like animals with bilateral symmetry.

Platyhelminthes—flat animals without a body cavity, such as flukes, tapeworms, and planaria and other flatworms.

Cnidaria—animals with radial symmetry and stinging cells, such as jellyfish, hydras, sea anemones, and corals.

Porifera—sponges, filter-feeding animals.

In this system, the more detailed the level of classification, the more specific the traits become. For example, dogs are classified in this way:

The Dog

Level		Characteristics
Kingdom	Animalia	Multicellular body, eukaryotic cells, eats food
Phylum	Chordata	Has nerve cord
Class	Mammalia	Hair on body, female produces milk for young
Order	Carnivora	Preys on other animals; eats meat
Family	Canidae	Large canine teeth; dog-like carnivores adapted to hunting
Genus	*Canis*	All wild dogs, including jackals, dingos, and wolves
Species	*familiaris*	Domesticated dogs

Plantae, the Plant Kingdom

The plant Kingdom is the second largest Kingdom. No one knows exactly how many species it includes. There could be as many as four hundred thousand individual species. Most plants are multicellular organisms that make their own food through photosynthesis. Green plants contain a light-sensitive pigment called chlorophyll. Chlorophyll enables the plant to make food using water, carbon dioxide, and energy from sunlight.

Biologists have several ways of classifying plants. The classification systems are changing as botanists learn more about plant genes. Botanists officially group plants into twelve Phyla, or divisions. Many botanists think of all the Phyla as being in one of these three unofficial categories—nonvascular seedless plants, vascular seedless plants, and vascular seed plants.

Oak leaf ▶

Maple leaves

Ivy leaf

Geranium leaves

33

Nonvascular seedless plants: These plants do not have any tubes for transporting water and nutrients. They also do not have seeds for reproduction. Nonvascular seedless plants are tiny and simple. There are three Phyla of these:

Bryophyta—mosses
Hepatophyta—liverworts
Anthocerophyta—hornworts

Vascular seedless plants: These plants have a system of transporting water from roots to the other parts of the plant. They do not reproduce with seeds. There are four Phyla of seedless vascular plants:

Pteridophyta—ferns
Equisetophyta—horsetails or scouring rushes
Psilophyta—whisk ferns
Lycopodiophyta—plants that have some features of a moss and some of a fern

Vascular seed plants: These are complex plants.

They have a system for transporting water and nutrients. They also reproduce through seeds.

There are two main types of vascular seed plants—gymnosperms and angiosperms. "Gymnosperm" is a term for the group of plants that produce seeds, but not flowers or fruit. There are four Phyla of gymnosperms:

Pinophyta (once called Coniferophyta)—cone-bearing plants, such as pine, fir, and spruce.
Cycadophyta—tropical plants that look like palms but produce huge cones.
Ginkgophyta—the ginko is a cone-producing tree with leaves instead of needles.
Gnetophyta—a tropical vine.

Angiosperm is a term used for all the flowering plants, including trees such as oak, apple, and maple. The flowering plants are the largest plant Phylum. It

Domains

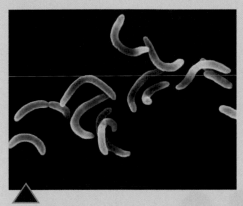

One-celled life-forms belong to the Bacteria Domain.

The current six-Kingdom classification system recognizes three groupings larger than Kingdoms. These groups are called Domains or "superkingdoms." The Domains are Eukarya, Bacteria, and Archaea.

Eukarya contains all those organisms whose cells have a nucleus. In eukaryotic cells, the cytoplasm, the gel-like matter inside the cells, has a central nucleus. It is enclosed in a nuclear membrane and contains the cell's genes.

Domain Eukarya includes the Animalia, Plantae, Fungi, and Protista Kingdoms.

Domain Bacteria contains all of the one-celled life-forms called bacteria. Bacterial cells do not have a nucleus. Cells without a nucleus are called prokaryotes. The DNA floats around in the cytoplasm.

Domain Archaea contains one-celled organisms that are also prokaryotes. Many of these archaeans live in extreme environments where ordinary bacteria or any other organism could not survive. Some live in boiling hot water or near sulfurous vents. Others thrive on poisonous substances, such as oil. Archaeans have some genes that are very different from genes in bacteria. Some archaean genes are more like genes in eukaryotes.

35

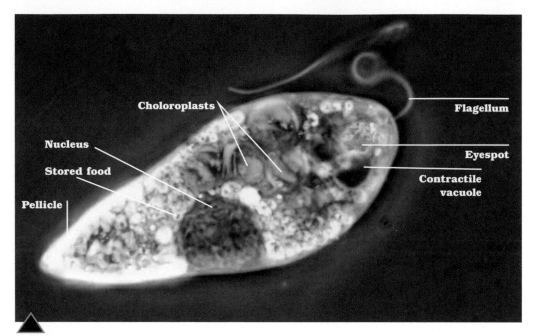

Choloroplasts

Nucleus

Stored food

Pellicle

Flagellum

Eyespot

Contractile
vacuole

Like a plant, the protist Euglena has chloroplasts to make its own food.

contains almost 250,000 species. There is only one Phylum of angiosperms.

The Fungi Kingdom

Botanists have identified about fifty thousand species in the Fungi Kingdom. Some fungi live in soil or water. Others are parasites. The best-known fungi sprout mushrooms. Yeasts, rust molds, and mildews are also fungi.

Fungi were once classified as plants. Unlike green plants, however, fungi cannot make chlorophyll. They cannot perform photosynthesis to make their food.

Protista, the Protist Kingdom

Most **protists** are one-celled organisms, but some are multicellular. All protists are eukaryotes.

Some protists take in food the way animals do. Amoebas are protists that were once thought to be tiny animals. They can push out feet-like projections called pseudopods that enable them to move around. Amoebas also surround food particles with their pseudopods and digest their food this way.

Some protists make food the way plants do. Algae, because they can contain chlorophyll, were once thought to be plants, but they are not. Algae can range in size from single-celled organisms to the graceful giant kelp.

There are many different classification systems for protists. In some systems of classification there are protist subkingdoms or superphyla.

Today, many biologists recognize three basic groups of protists. These are called protozons, algae, and slime or water molds. Slime molds were once classified as types of fungi.

Red Tides

Biologists are working to discover the caus of red tides and how to predict them.

Red tides are algal "blooms" caused by an increase in the number of dinoflagellates. Red tides kill fish and other sea creatures in oceans all over the world. The increase in algae can block sunlight, causing bacteria to multiply. They make the levels of oxygen in the water decrease dramatically. Also, algae, such as dinoflagellates, give off a toxin (poison). The toxin can kill small animals that eat the algae— as well as bigger animals that eat the smaller ones.

Protozoans

Protozoan means "pre-animal." Some biologists believe that multicellular animals evolved from these microscopic one-celled organisms. Protozoans include amoebas and ciliates such as paramecium.

Paramecium are covered with hairlike cilia used for movement and trapping food particles. The Euglena is a protozoan that has one whiplike hair, called a flagellum, that it uses to propel itself through water.

Some protozoans can cause serious diseases. Malaria, for example, is caused by a protozoan of the Species *Plasmodia*. This protozoan is transmitted to humans through the bite of a mosquito.

Algae

Algae live mostly in water. Green, brown, and red algae contain chlorophyll. Like plants, these algae can make their own food through photosynthesis. There are more than seven thousand species of green algae. There are about fifteen hundred species of brown algae, including such seaweeds as the giant kelp. There are more than four thousand species of red algae.

Most algae are one-celled organisms. Diatoms are a

Slime molds can take over an old piece of bread.

kind of microscopic algae with hard coverings made of a mineral found in sand. Diatoms grow in fresh and saltwater. They have many delicate shapes.

Dinoflagellates are one-celled organisms with two flagella. Some microscopic algae are poisonous to fish and other water organisms.

Plankton

Protozoans and algae are very important to the planet's food chain. These organisms, along with tiny animals, are part of the plankton that floats on the ocean. Plankton is an important food source for small animals that live in the sea and are, in turn, eaten by larger animals. The humpback whale and other baleen whales also eat plankton. Baleen whales have special parts in their mouths that can strain plankton out of seawater.

Slime Molds

Slime molds are fungus-like protists that live in decayed matter. They can be bright orange or yellow. They can have a powdery brown crust.

Unlike algae, they do not make food. They take in bacteria from their surroundings. Slime molds are big blobs of cytoplasm. The cells of some slime molds can group together and move around like amoebas by projecting pseudopods. The nuclei of other slime molds can come together to make a kind of "supercell" with many nuclei.

Changing Classification

Classification systems keep changing. They change as scientists learn more about living things. In the past, taxonomists had one way of classifying organisms. They grouped them only by such physical features as eyes, wings, and leaf structure. This older system helped identify organisms.

As scientists learned more about evolution, however, taxonomists began classifying organisms based on whether or not they evolved from a common ancestor. The classification of organisms according to their evolutionary history is called phylogeny. Taxonomists also think about the relationships among organisms. They study how embryos evolve, for instance.

They learn what features the embryos have at different stages of development. The new methods help with understanding evolution.

Classifications Constantly Change

Classifying organisms is a constant challenge. Biologists continue to find new specimens. A major new group of insects, called an Order, was discovered in the early 2000s in southern Africa. It was the first such group discovered since the early 1900s. The insects in the new Order are somewhat like a stick insect, a mantid, and a grasshopper—yet different from all three. The discovery brought the number of insect Orders to thirty-one.

🔑 Pronunciation Key:

archaea (are-KEE-ah)

bryophtya
(BRYE-ih-fite)

chlorophyll
(KLOR-oh-fill)

chordate (KORE-date)

embryo (EM-bree-oh)

eubacteria
(YOU-bak-TEAR-ee-ah)

eukaryote (you-KARE-ee-oat)

ginkgophyta
(GHING-koh-fite-ah)

hepatophyta
(heh-pah-TOE-fite-ah)

phylogeny
(fye-LAH-juh-knee)

prokaryote
(pro-KARE-ee-oat)

Adaptation and Super Bugs

Antibiotics are drugs that kill living organisms that cause diseases. The first antibiotic, penicillin, was discovered in 1928 by Scottish doctor Alexander Fleming. In 1943, drug companies began to produce penicillin. More powerful antibiotics followed. Before these "wonder drugs" were invented, many diseases caused by bacteria, such as pneumonia, tuberculosis, and various kinds of infections, were often fatal.

Patients often demand antibiotics from doctors, even for colds and other viral infections—which antibiotics cannot help. Antibiotics were added to farm animal feed. For a time, drug companies stopped looking for new antibiotics. Then, something began to go wrong.

By the 1980s, public health officials noticed that antibiotics no longer worked against some kinds of pneumonia and other infections. The disease-causing bacteria had evolved to become resistant to the antibiotic medications.

Here is what happened: A small number of bacteria developed genes that were resistant to an antibiotic. The drugs did not kill the resistant bacteria. These bacteria reproduced and began to replace the bacteria that were not drug resistant. Even worse, these bacteria could "swap" their resistant genes with other bacteria.

By the 1990s, drug resistant bacteria had become a serious problem. Drug manufacturers are searching for new types of antibiotics. Farmers stopped including antibiotics in feed. Doctors must be sure that the antibiotics they prescribe are really necessary.

Glossary

adaptation an adjustment to conditions; any modification in an organism that makes it better able to survive

amino acid one of the chemical building blocks of proteins

amoeba a one-celled animal-like organism classified as a protist

atom the smallest unit of a chemical element

bacterium a one-celled organism that lacks a nucleus

camouflage to blend in with one's surroundings for protection against predators

carbohydrate a sugar or starch produced by plants and consumed as food by animals

carbon dioxide a gas in air given off as a waste product by animals and used by plants

cell the smallest whole unit of a living organism

cladogram a diagram showing how living organisms are related to one another

crystal a nonliving solid with an internal structure that can form a pleasing appearance

DNA (deoxyribonucleic acid) the molecule of which genes are made

embryo the earliest stage of a plant or animal's life

environment the surroundings in which an organism lives

eukaryote a cell with a nucleus containing DNA

evolution the development of one species from another over a long period of time

fossil remains or imprint of a once-living organism

fossil fuels substances, such as coal, oil, or natural gas, that formed from prehistoric plants and animals

genes pieces of DNA that carry the codes for proteins

Genus a classification category above Species but below Family

gravity a force that pulls one object toward another

hibernation an inactive state

hierarchical a ranking of things in levels from greater to lesser

hormones proteins that regulate systems in plants and animals

humidity the amount of water vapor in the air

hypotheses interpretations of a condition or situation

invertebrate an animal without a backbone

Kingdom one of the primary classification categories above Phylum but below Domain

maggots larvae of a fly

microscope instrument consisting of one or more lenses for making tiny objects look larger

mimicry taking on the appearance or behavior of a harmful organism for protection against predators

molecule atoms joined together to create a substance

nonvascular plants that do not have a system for transporting water and nutrients

organic material containing the element carbon

organisms living things

oxygen a gas in the air needed by animals and given off as a waste product by plants

photosynthesis a process by which plants and some algae make food from water and carbon dioxide using the energy of sunlight

prey an animal hunted by another animal for food

prokaryotes cells that do not have a nucleus

proteins building blocks of cells also needed for all cell functions

protists simple animal-like life-forms

Species a basic level in the scientific classification system

taxonomy the classification of organisms and other things according to a set of rules

vascular having a tubelike system for transporting water and nutrients

vertebrates animals with backbones

viruses capsules of simple genes inside a protein coat that infects cells and directs the cell to make copies of the virus

For More Information

Books

Anderson, Margaret Jean.
Carl Linnaeus: Father of Classification.
Enslow (1997)

Clark, Edward, and John Ownes.
Scientific Classification, Vol. 9.
Scholastic (2002)

Protists and Fungi.
Gareth Stevens (2003)

Fullick, Ann.
Variation and Classification.
Heinemann (2006)

Human, Katy (editor).
*Biological Evolution: An Anthology
of Current Thought.*
Rosen Central (2005)

Morgan, Jennifer.
*Mammals Who Morph:
The Universe Tells Our Evolution Story.*
Dawn Publications (2006)

Sloan, Christopher.
*How Dinosaurs Took Flight: The Fossils,
the Science, What We Think We Know,
and Mysteries Yet Unsolved.*
National Geographic (2005)

Thomas, Peggy.
Bacteria and Viruses.
Thomson Gale(2004)

Web Sites

www.fi.edu/tfi/units/life/
Take a detailed look at individual
organisms, groupings, and life cycles.

*commtechlab.msu.edu/sites/
dlc-me/zoo/*
Take trip to a virtual zoo and discover
the millions of microbes—good and
bad—that live in and on you.

*oceanlink.island.net/oinfo/seaweeds/
seaweeds.html*
Learn interesting facts about seaweed.

*www.usoe.k12.ut.us/curr/science/
sciber00/7th/classify/living/2.htm*
Test your knowledge with quizzes or try
some activities that accompany these
easy-to-follow explanations of the basic
functions of living things.

*www.saburchill.com/chapters/chap0001
.html*
Check out these facts, figures, quizzes,
and tables.

Publisher's note to educators and parents: Our
editors have carefully reviewed these Web sites to
ensure that they are suitable for children. Many
Web sites change frequently, however, and we
cannot guarantee that a site's future contents will
continue to meet our high standards of quality
and educational value. Be advised that children
should be closely supervised whenever they
access the Internet.

Index